THE POACHER'S MOON

Richard Peirce

Published by:
Shark Cornwall, Dulverton House, Crooklets,
Bude, Cornwall, EX23 8NE, United Kingdom

First published: 2013
© Richard Peirce, Shark Cornwall.

ISBN no. 978-0-9558694-5-7

Photographs: Jacqui Peirce and as indicated
Design and Artwork: SR Print Management Ltd
Printed and bound in England by
SR Print Management Limited, Newmarket 2 Centrix Keys,
Keys Park Road, Hednesford, WS12 2HA, United Kingdom

– – – – –

SOON TO BE PUBLISHED BY THE SAME AUTHOR
"Shark Adventures – the expeditions"

OTHER PRODUCTS
"Sharks in British Seas" – Book (Shark Cornwall)
"Sharks in British Seas" – DVD (Elasmo Films)
"Sharks off Cornwall and Devon" – Book (Tor Mark Publishing)
"Shark Attack Britain" – DVD (Shark Bay Films)
"Pirates of Devon & Cornwall" – Book (Shark Cornwall)
"Execution Sites of Devon & Cornwall" – Book (Shark Cornwall)

All books and DVD's can be bought through the website
www.sharkconservationsociety.com

RHINO FACTS

- White rhinos shoulder height is up to 1.8 metres
- White rhinos can weigh up to approx 3,500 kg
- White rhinos can run at speeds up to 40 k.p.h
- Rhino horn is made of keratin
- Rhino horn will re-grow at a rate of 6/10cm per annum
- The gestation period for rhinos is 15/18 months
- Rhino calves weigh between 45/65 kg at birth
- There are five species of rhino, the Indian, Sumatran, Javan, and African black and white rhinos
- The Sumatran rhino is the smallest of the five
- It is believed that the last rhino in Southern Java was shot in 1934
- The last captive Javan rhino died in Adelaide zoo in 1907
- Rhino horn is now worth more than gold at over $65,000 per kilo
- Rhinos have been on planet earth for over 50 million years
- Depending on species rhino live for between 30 and 60 years
- The name rhinoceros comes from the Greek rhino (nose) and ceros (horn)
- A group of rhinos is called a crash
- The white rhino is the second largest land species after the elephant
- Rhinos leave piles of dung as messages for other rhino
- Rhinos are related to horses and zebras
- Rhinos are herbivores (vegetarians)
- Humans are the most dangerous predator for rhinos

USEFUL WEBSITES

Adopt a rhino   www.wwf.org.uk/adopt_rhino

Black Rhino Conservation   www.actforwildlife.org.uk

Born Free Foundation   www.bornfree.org

CITES   www.cites.org

International Rhino Foundation   www.rhinos-irf.org

Project rhino   www.projectrhinokzn.org

Protect rhino in South Africa   www.globalgiving.co.uk

Rhino conservation   www.sheldrickwildlifetrust.org

Rhino Protect   www.rhinoprotect.org

Saving Private Rhino   www.savingprivaterhino.org

Save the rhino   www.savetherhino.org

Stop rhino poaching   www.stoprhinopoaching.com

TRAFFIC (wildlife trade monitoring)   www.traffic.org

WWF   www.wwf.org.uk

THE POACHER'S MOON

This book is dedicated to Higgins
and Lady and all the rhinos, dead
and alive, which have been attacked
by poachers. It is also dedicated to
the brave men and women who work
on the front line trying to protect
animals – some of whom have been
killed doing their jobs. We owe it to
the dead humans and rhinos to develop
effective conservation measures to
ensure the survival of the remaining
rhino species in the wild.

The Poacher's Moon

CHAPTER 1 – LIMPOPO DAWN, LIFE BEGINS

Small smoke like puffs of dust rose from the ground with every footfall as the huge grey prehistoric-looking creature made its way silently across the moonlit African landscape.

The female southern white rhino was sixteen months pregnant and ready to give birth. She had a rounded look to her and her belly swung slightly as she walked. Her calf would only weigh 45-65 kg, so even at full term would be a relatively small foetus compared to its mother's massive three and a half tonne bulk.

A week ago she had chased off her two year old calf in preparation for the new arrival. The moon reflected a perfect shadow of her as she walked slowly across the flat sandy area heading for the cover of some trees and bushes a couple of hundred metres away. At the front of the shadow were two magnificent horns which rose to sharp points. It was a full moon, sometimes known as a poacher's moon, and later on a poacher's moon would play a major part in the life of her new calf.

After chasing off her two year old calf the cow rhino had left her *crash and gone in search of a quiet place to give birth. Her horn pushed the branches aside, and she walked in and out of the moonlight making her way through the shadows cast by the bushes and trees. She entered a small area of clear ground which had a slight depression in one corner. She circled the little clearing stopping often to listen and sniff the air. Apparently satisfied, she lay down in the shallow depression, found a lump of wood and started to chew it.

Two hours later, lying on her side, she gave birth to a 50 kg male calf which arrived with a wet, squelchy gurgling sound. The baby southern white rhino, which would one day become world famous, and be known as Higgins, had made his undignified entry into the world. Higgins was standing on his wobbly legs within an hour and was trying to suckle very soon after. His was an experienced mother who helped manoeuvre him into position, and by the time he was two hours old he was steady on his legs and feeding contentedly.

For the next two months Higgins and his mother were rarely more than a few feet apart, and very often he was in front of his mother and appeared to be leading the way. Higgins started grazing at three months and by now mother and calf were often in the company of other rhino in their *crash.   *(*crash – a group of rhino)*

When Higgins was born in 2000 the population of southern white rhino had recovered from near extinction. There were only a few hundred in 1900, rising to about 19,000 in 2000 mostly in South Africa. Higgins was born in the north of South Africa's Limpopo Province, only a few kilometres from the border with Botswana.

Four years later in the southern Kruger National Park a female calf was born whose life would eventually become entwined with that of Higgins and who would also become an unwitting global celebrity. She would later be known as Lady and coincidentally she was also born under a full moon.

When Higgins was five years old he was loaded into a specially adapted truck and, under the watchful eye of a vet, was driven 1500 kilometres to his new home on the Fairy Glen Game Reserve. He was happy enough in his new surroundings but a single rhino looked strange and lonely and in 2010 Fairy Glen's owner, Pieter de Jager, bought a female companion for Higgins.

Lady, now aged six, arrived at the reserve in late 2010 and the pair quickly became inseparable. They grazed together, walked and mud bathed together, slept side by side, and a year after Lady had arrived they were seen mating.

The de Jager family bought Fairy Glen in the early 1970's. The farm is overlooked by the Auden mountain which is part of the

Brandwacht range and towers to a height of 5331 ft to the north of the main farm buildings. There is snow on the mountains in the winter and Fairy Glen was once a ski resort. Some of today's guest safari lodges are yesterday's converted ski chalets.

The farm was a vineyard when the de Jagers bought it forty years ago, but was not ideally suited to growing grapes. The family made the farm work in various other ways and grazed sheep, reared cattle, and grew crops until in 2000 Pieter de Jager converted Fairy Glen into a game reserve and opened it to the public.

Pieter believes that the last white rhino in the Western Cape was shot and killed in 1691 on what is now Fairy Glen. The trigger was pulled by Simon van der Stel who was the first governor of the Cape Colony. If this story is true there is a gap of 314 years until Higgins arrived and rhinos once again lived in the shadow of the Auden mountain. Fairy Glen is a small reserve which is largely covered by fynbos (natural shrubland), grass fields, scrub and some woodland. The Lodge is situated 2 kilometres up a track from the main gate and occupies a wonderful position overlooking the dam, which means that guests have a continual view of animals as they come to drink. Despite its small size, Fairy Glen is home to 17 species, and the de Jagers hoped that their rhinos would breed and further add to the appeal of the reserve. By the time Higgins and Lady began their life together at Fairy Glen in 2010 rhino poaching had once again become a scourge which was starting to threaten the survival of the species.

Higgins and Lady before the attack   *copyright Fairy Glen*

Fairy Glen's main gate   *copyright Jacqui Peirce*

The Poacher's Moon

CHAPTER 2 – ATTACK ON AQUILA

The Aquila game reserve lies just off the N1, 10 kms to the west of Touwsrivier. It is a commercially successful reserve handling over 60,000 visitors a year. The visitors are a mixture of overnight guests and day visitors who are largely tourists from Cape Town, which is less than two hours away by road. The other game reserves which are within a couple of hours drive from Cape Town are Fairy Glen and Inverdoorn. All three reserves can lay claim to being home to Africa's Big 5 – elephant, rhino, lion, buffalo and leopard - but leopard occur infrequently and visitors are very lucky to see one. Of the Big 5 species on the reserves buffalo, rhino and leopard are free roaming, whereas elephant are often kept in bomas and lion in small separate fenced reserves.

There are people who criticise such relatively small reserves and call them fenced farms or large zoos. However, the other side of the coin is that they give visitors an opportunity to see Africa's main game species only a short drive from the tourist magnet that is Cape Town. Most visitors don't have the time, opportunity, or inclination to go to the Kruger or the Kgalagadi Transfrontier Park, or drive to Etosha in Namibia, or the Okavango Delta in Botswana, and these smaller, tamer alternatives provide a taste of African wildlife.

The Aquila Game Reserve is the brainchild of owner Searl Derman and opened for business in 1999. The first rhino, a male, arrived in 2002 and was nicknamed ABSA after the bank that advanced the money to buy him. Further animals were acquired and by August 2011 there were six rhinos on the reserve.

Saturday August 20th 2011 began like any other day for Searl Derman when he woke at his home in Cape Town. Then at 9.00 a.m. he answered a call on his cellphone and the blood felt as if it was freezing in his veins. A year earlier a lawyer friend of his from Johannesburg had warned him that the rhinos at Aquila were a target for poachers. Now the nightmare was happening: the call was from the reserve and told him his rhinos had been attacked by poachers.

The earlier warning from his lawyer only confirmed what Searl already knew – it was just a matter of time before his animals would be poached. He had bought weapons and applied for licences, but the weapons remained in store as the licences had not come through. Perhaps this was a blessing, because had his rangers been armed and come across the poachers there would have been a fire fight with the possibility of human deaths on both sides. There is evidence that the rangers did, albeit unwittingly, disturb the poachers who broke off their attack and fled.

Searl drove up the N1 towards Aquila as fast as he could. The call had told him he had two rhinos missing, and another fighting for its life. He realised his two priorities were to try and save the injured rhinos, and organise a search for the missing animals, which might also be injured or dead. He stopped in Paarl to try and pick up some antidote to the anaesthetic dart that would have been used, but couldn't find the right one. He phoned his vet who advised him to get the human equivalent, and he ended up jumping over a pharmacy counter, grabbing as much as he could, paying, and leaving to continue his dash to Aquila. The journey from hell hadn't finished because at some time he hit bumps going over the veldt and the door of his vehicle locked, temporarily trapping him inside.

He reached the reserve just after 11.30 a.m. and walked into a maelstrom of activity that badly needed organising and directing. Vets had already arrived but they were small animal vets with no experience of rhino. ABSA, the male rhino, had had a horn hacked off and was stumbling around in a tormented daze. There were cuts on the second horn, but it was still on the animal with part of a saw blade broken off in the wound. This, and other evidence that would come to light later, pointed to the poachers having been disturbed during their raid.

Searl's first priority was to get the antidote into the rhino. ABSA was something of a celebrity as he was the first rhino reintroduced into the Western Cape since they were hunted to local extinction decades before. Injecting antidote is a dangerous business even when the subject is half dazed and injured as ABSA was. Searl waited his chance and injected him in the rump. Despite having one injured leg the rhino stayed on his feet. He quickly seemed brighter and hopes for his survival increased.

Searl now turned his attention to organising the search for the missing animals, hoping against hope that he wouldn't find them dead with their faces hacked off, bleeding and dying. Quad bikes, horses, vehicles and helicopters were all searching the veldt for the missing rhinos. The first was found stumbling around in a wooded area. She was ABSA's daughter and had been darted but still had her horns, which was further evidence that the poachers had fled before finishing their work.

Searl kept her attention, allowing the vet to approach from behind and administer the antidote. Two animals had now been successfully injected with the antidote. One was injured and the other not, but there was nothing more Searl could do for either at the moment, so he took to a helicopter to search for the last missing rhino.

They spotted a still, grey body lying in a gully with a pool of blood around its head and a pile of dung at its rear. With the syringe in his hand Searl leapt from the helicopter as soon as it touched down and sprinted to the inert grey mass. Even as he ran he knew he was too late, the rhino was dead, the huge amount of blood and the bowel evacuation were sure signs. The dead rhino was discovered just after 1.00 p.m. only four hours after Searl had received the call to his Cape Town home. What had started as a normal day would probably end up being the most abnormal day of his life.

The morning had also started normally for those on the early game drive who had discovered the stricken ABSA, and raised the alarm that the reserve had been attacked. A vehicle full of ordinary tourists looking forward to seeing some of Africa's wildlife suddenly found themselves on the frontline of the war against poaching. The awful reality of rhino poaching is cruelty, suffering, blood and death, and the images the tourists saw that day will remain with them for a long time. They had seen what humans will do to other animals for money.

Searl had six rhinos – one had been killed, one had been saved by the antidote, and ABSA was critically ill. When he had gone down after being darted he had lain on rocks on one leg for too long. He now not only had half his face missing, he had a badly damaged leg due to his blood circulation having been restricted and his ability to move was limited. This meant he couldn't regulate his body temperature by seeking shade or a mud bath if he got hot at midday, and at night he could get too cold if in an exposed place. Attempts to get him to drink from manmade puddles and buckets had been largely unsuccessful. On day three ABSA had to be darted again to get a fluid drip into him for a couple of hours. Afterwards, when giving the antidote, Searl nearly killed himself. The quantity of fluid to be injected was large and the only syringe big enough was a plastic one. The vet had failed trying to get the drug in and Searl made a last desperate attempt. It worked and he got quite a lot injected, but the syringe broke and the rest ended up in his face. He thought it was over but keeping calm and a bucket of water over his face saved his life. Luckily he was still working with the human antidote, the rhino one would have killed him.

ABSA managed to move short distances but was immobile most of the time. Crows sensed he was in trouble and came to peck at his eyes, and there were fears that, if left unattended, buffalo, leopard and elephant would all pose threats.

Rhino can make an almost human crying noise, and many times during these difficult days the sounds ABSA made brought tears to his carer's eyes. ABSA's daughter was distressed by her father's plight and tried to get near to comfort and lie down next to him. The presence of a fully fit very troubled young rhino made the work of ABSA's carers even more dangerous: she tried to protect her father by preventing Searl and his team getting close to him.

To win the battle for ABSA's life Searl had to create an intensive care unit, and do so in a protected zone to restrict ABSA's movement, and prevent interference from other animals. He decided to use a big lorry like an F250 or a Dodge with a large robust trailer, a crane and a cradle, and ultrasound equipment to massage the injured leg. He brought in five forty-foot containers which could be circled to create a safe area in which it would be easy to make shade. By now it was the fifth day after the attack, and Searl and all those at Aquila were confident ABSA would make it.

The carers sat up watching him as usual throughout the night on day five, but when the dawn broke for the sixth time since the attack the team realised he had died. They had done everything they could to save his life but it hadn't been enough.

The poachers had darted three rhino and in the end only one had survived. Police trackers and dogs had worked the whole area and found a lot of signs left by the attackers. The poachers had watched the reserve for several days from observation posts (OP's), and knew exactly where the rhinos were likely to be at any time of the day or night. When they attacked they had worked in two teams, one of two people and the other of three. They had darted three of six rhinos before being disturbed. It is likely their intention had been to poach the horns of all six animals which they would have achieved had they not been interrupted.

The N1 highway is only 2 kms to the southeast of Aquila. Between the reserve and the highway there is only one farm. The police followed the trail left by the poachers as they fled, and

Continued on page 21

Searl Derman

The poachers were interrupted and left ABSA with part of his horn

copyright Aquila game reserve

The fight to save ABSA

Searl Derman despairs as he mourns his rhino and confronts the brutal reality of poaching

ABSA lost his fight for life after five days

copyright Aquila

The poachers dropped a jersey as they fled

copyright Aquila

found a jersey and a glove dropped on the ground. They also found where the fence had been cut at their exit point. All the poachers then had to do was cover the few hundred metres of farmland and they could speed off east or west on the highway.

At 2013 prices the value of the horn from all six Aquila rhinos would have been well over 2 million US dollars (circa 20 million rand), so it's easy to see why private reserves were starting to become increasingly popular targets. In the Kruger National Park highly trained rangers, often armed with automatic weapons and sometimes working with Special Forces, were life-threatening opponents. The poacher's expectation would have been that small private reserves would be less lethal and less well prepared.

The news of the Aquila attack spread fast and it became a global story largely due to ABSA's heroic fight for life. The neighbouring reserves of Inverdoorn and Fairy Glen hastily increased their patrols and security.

The poachers had got away with it, and although they left with only three out of a possible twelve horns, it was still a profitable night's work. Pieter de Jager at Fairy Glen, and Damien Vergnaud at Inverdoorn, both realised the poaching gang would be frustrated yet emboldened by their experience at Aquila.

Searl Derman still had four rhinos left, so he kept up his security, brought in extra trained men and, once the permits arrived, issued his rangers with weapons. The problems of the Kruger Park hundreds of miles to the northeast were now part of the daily lives of all those on the three Western Cape reserves.

Searl Derman is on record criticising the length of time it took to issue his weapons licences. He believes that if his rangers had actually walked into the poachers they wouldn't have been able to defend themselves and would have been shot. He is also on record being critical of the police investigation which followed the raid. Derman claims it was months before the police interviewed him, which was very frustrating because he had several ideas regarding possible suspects. While waiting for police action he conducted his own investigations which resulted in his handing over names and information to the police. During our interview Searl talked of arrests he had facilitated, which involved seizures of shark fins, ivory and rhino horns. Despite these successes no-one has yet been arrested for the attack on Aquila and his frustration remains.

He informed me the reason the police gave him for not acting was that they were working to try and break poaching rings operating on a national level. He says he was told his case forms part of a body of evidence being collected, and that if the police moved too early they might blow their chances of convicting the major criminal gangs ....time will be the judge!

The Poacher's Moon

CHAPTER 3 – THE POACHER'S MOON

The men cast clear shadows on the ground as they crept through
the bush. Glinting dully in the full moon were the rifle and the
*pangas they carried. A twig snapped and the leader's head
whipped round as he silently cursed his noisy accomplice. The light
was so good the three poachers felt very exposed as they were in
plain view of the Fairy Glen Lodge only five hundred metres away.
Higgins slept as Lady snuffled in the dust a little to his left. She
heard the men and turned to face the direction of their approach.
Perfect shadows of Lady's horns were cast on the sand, and she
snorted and stamped nervously. Her fear transmitted itself to
Higgins who woke and got to his feet ready to defend himself and
his mate. The rhinos had no chance, the rifle spat and the first dart
flew true to its mark and buried itself in Higgins shoulder. M99 is
the anaesthetic drug used by vets to put animals to sleep when they
need to administer treatment or move them; it is also widely used
by poachers. A second dart followed the first and again found its

(panga, similar to a machete, a large African knife)

23

target and pumped its deadly contents into the rhino. Higgins instincts were confused, charge his attackers or run? He ran, expecting Lady to follow.

The gunman was quick, he reloaded and hit Lady just as Higgins wheeled to flee. Lady made the other decision and started to charge, then changed her mind and turned to follow Higgins. Her legs had stopped working and she collapsed having staggered only three steps. Higgins was ninety metres away when the drug overcame his massive strength and his nervous system gave up. Forward momentum propelled him into a ditch and as he lost consciousness he realised he was alone. Lady was not with him. The moon's silver silence was broken only by the laboured breathing of the two stricken rhinos.

The men stood absolutely still waiting to see if the shots and the noise made by the rhinos would produce a reaction from the lodge. They waited only two minutes before deciding to go to work. Two hacked at the base of Lady's horns with their pangas, while the third sprinted to the ditch where Higgins lay. The male rhino had been given twice the dose needed, his heart had slowed and his breathing was shallow as the first panga cut bit into his head. Higgins attacker was near panic; his two friends were together dealing with Lady while he was working alone. His nervousness pushed him to the edge of terror, and he hacked Higgins horn in a mad frenzy of brutality. He missed the base of the horn, hit live tissue and blood crept from the wound then spurted high as his next blow deepened the cut.

Cocky and confident now, the two poachers had finished with Lady and walked, almost strolled, to join the third man with Higgins in the ditch. One had the rifle slung over his shoulder and on the other's back bounced a sack containing Lady's horn. Higgins head was covered in blood, one horn was gone and blood bubbled where the poacher had hacked so deep he had gone into his sinuses. The leader pushed his man roughly aside and took over work on the remaining horn.

Two hundred metres away the eland woke, sensed danger, panicked and crashed away through the bush. Startled the men looked up, then three more powerful panga cuts and Higgins second horn came free.

The poachers gathered their prizes, and forgot silence as they ran to the fence to leave. They had come equipped with wire cutters and were soon through the wire and on their way. They had left Higgins dying in the ditch and ran past Lady without a glance.

The rhinos had been easy targets, a day earlier a bush fire had been deliberately started to the northeast of Fairy Glen. The helicopter pilot who dropped water on the fire had been able to identify the four places where it had been lit with petrol. Animals will always move away from fire, and so it was that Higgins and Lady were down at the southwest end of the reserve that night only a hundred metres from the fence. A farm track runs along the outside of the fence and the poachers had left their vehicle close to where they knew they would cut the wire and flee. They had attacked just after 3 a.m. Less than half an hour later they walked back the few hundred metres to the fence and then to their waiting vehicle. They drove to the west and were most of the way home when the sun rose over Fairy Glen and exposed their grisly night's work.

———————

To the northeast of Fairy Glen is Inverdoorn, another private game reserve. Inverdoorn's owner, Damien Vergnaud, hadn't slept well. Ever since the attack on Aquila and the killing of their animals Damien had worried about his rhinos. Several times during the night he had got out of bed and gone to the window to look at the moonlit landscape. As dawn broke and Higgins and Lady fought for their lives Damien shuddered without knowing why. In a few hours his phone would ring, his life would change forever, and he wouldn't sleep for many nights.

———————

Pieter De Jager will never forget Sunday 11th December 2011. At ten past seven his cell phone rang and Jan the reserve manager poured out a torrent of words that seemed to make no sense. Lady, attacked, poached, dying, blood, Higgins, disappeared, were all jumbled up, then came together bringing their clear and terrible message. Jan had been driving into the reserve giving Willem de

Wee a lift to work. Willem had looked to his left and seen Lady on her side with her legs in the air.

Pieter was in his vehicle within minutes and driving the 9 km from his home to Fairy Glen. As he drove he called the police, his vet, and his friend Johan Botma. He asked Johan, better known as Bottie, to meet him at Fairy Glen as soon as he could. His son, young Pieter, had turned 10 yesterday and the family had held a party at the reserve. He was driving in a vehicle still filled with yesterday's birthday balloons towards a nightmare: it seemed insane and surreal.

Nausea and fear wouldn't help his rhinos if they were still alive, so he tried to put his feelings to one side as he drove, and wondered why time always seems to pass slowly when you are in a hurry. If the gate to the reserve had been closed Pieter would probably have crashed through it, he didn't even notice it was open as he raced past the entrance.

Pieter ran towards Lady, fearful of what he would find. Chantelle, a Fairy Glen ranger, was on her knees next to Lady, crying and begging her "Don't die". Those words meant she was still alive, and as Pieter realised this he changed. Fear, horror, nausea and despair were replaced by an ice cold anger and a steely determination that Lady would not die. He wouldn't let her die, he couldn't let her die, because if he did the poachers would have won. He saw that her breathing was irregular and weak, and both of her horns had been gouged out with cuts that had gone into her sinus passages. Chantelle continually wiped out Lady's nose to help her breathing.

"Where's the bull, where is Higgins?" The voice belonged to Bottie and hearing it added to Pieter's growing determination and confidence. Lady lay still but her eyes were open and Bottie quickly instructed they be covered to protect against sun damage. Many people have a particular good friend they would want by their side in a crisis. For Pieter it is his school friend Bottie, who now strode towards where Lady lay, calmly issuing advice and instructions. The area of flat ground below the lodge had become a hive of activity. Wet towels arrived and were placed over Lady's eyes and two rangers ran around working a search pattern looking for Higgins. It was Sunday so Pieter hadn't been able to speak to his vet, he had only been able to leave a message. Pieter and Bottie realised they would have to deal with this themselves and act quickly if they were going to save Lady's life. The wound needed cleaning and sealing, an antidote had to be administered, and antibiotics and dressings were needed fast. The minutes ticked away as Pieter and Bottie worked their cellphones, searching for what would save their animal.

Continued page 32

Fire at the Reserve a day before the attack *copyright Fairy Glen*

Pieter de Jager *copyright Fairy Glen*

Chantelle was begging Lady not to die

Bottie and Pieter injecting Lady with the antidote Narcan

Game ranger Riaan removes two darts from Lady *copyright Fairy Glen*

Lady responds to the antidote and struggles to her feet

copyright Fairy Glen

Continued from page 28

"I'll go to the local hospital, we'll have to try human antidote, it's our only chance", Bottie was yelling backwards over his shoulder to Pieter as he ran to his vehicle. The local hospital is several kilometres away and Bottie went at it like a Formula 1 driver. Johan Botma stands well over six feet tall, has long hair tied back in a ponytail and weighs over 135 kilos. He is a large kind man with a huge heart. That morning as he burst into Worcester hospital he didn't look at all kind or genial, and nothing was going to stop him getting the drugs that might give Lady a chance. The hospital staff were immediately sympathetic and helpful, and minutes after he had arrived he was leaving the hospital again with its entire supply of Narcan, the human antidote, tucked in a box under his arm.

Bottie's absence was an eternity for Pieter, although in fact he was back in just over half an hour. Pieter prayed as he injected the antidote into the soft skin and the vein behind Lady's ear. They were worried that if she lay in her unnatural position much longer she might damage her organs. An ear twitched, then both ears moved and her breathing started to sound stronger and become more regular.

"Over here, over here, he is here, Higgins is here". Pieter and Bottie would never describe themselves as athletes but they covered the 100 metres to the frantically waving ranger in seconds. The male rhino was in a ditch which was why they had not seen him before. Bad though Lady's wounds were, they were not as bad as Higgins'. The frenzied hacking had gone deeper into his sinuses and blood frothed and bubbled as he struggled to breathe. The sun's rays were doing awful damage to Higgins open and unprotected eyes. Rhinos don't have good eyesight, and as Bottie gently placed a wet towel over Higgins eyes he wondered if he might not already be too late and Higgins would be blind - if he survived.

Pieter didn't hear the vehicle approach, but Dr. Belstead his vet had arrived and immediately took over tending to Higgins. "We'll need Stockholm Tar and lots of it to seal the wounds". It was Sunday so the local agricultural store was closed and going to Cape Town would take too long. Fate or God started to take a hand, and just as Pieter began to despair another vet called saying he had enough Stockholm Tar for both rhinos. Bottie and the vet worked hard and within a few minutes Higgins had been injected with the antidote M50, painkillers, antibiotics and vitamins. As with Lady, the ears moved first then he struggled to lift his mutilated head, Pieter, Bottie and their vet watched as their brave patient regained consciousness.

The sun was high by 11.00 o'clock and the scene was something of a circus as the police, Cape Nature investigators, and the forensic team went about their work.

The media were starting to arrive in numbers and the melee was joined by the specialised crime unit, The Hawks. For Pieter, Bottie and the Fairy Glen rangers the investigation was of secondary importance, what mattered to them was saving their rhinos, and that battle had only just begun.

Higgins is found in a ditch

Bottie and Higgins in the ditch

Dr. Bellstead treats Higgins' mutilated face   *copyright Fairy Glen*

In the end Higgins was able to walk out of the ditch unaided without needing the
lifting and construction equipment that had been assembled   *copyright Fairy Glen*

Higgins eyes were protected from the sun with a wet towel   *copyright Fairy Glen*

Higgins got to his feet without help   *copyright Fairy Glen*

Bottie points to where Lady was lying   *copyright Jacqui Peirce*

At the fence where the poachers made their escape   *copyright Jacqui Peirce*

CONSERVATION QUESTIONS AND ISSUES

There isn't one answer to the conservation of earth's wildlife, there are several, and they need implementing quickly. If, in past decades, wildlife NGO's, the IUCN, and CITES had been operating effectively we wouldn't be looking again at the rhino becoming extinct in the wild, the IUCN Red List (threatened species) wouldn't be as long as it is, and elephant poaching wouldn't be back on the agenda, etc. There are no simple answers, and excellent work has been done, but slowly the battle for earth's wildlife is being lost.

Organisations like CITES are sound ideas but they need real teeth to enable them to operate effectively. Around the world there are thousands of wildlife NGO's spending billions of dollars. How effective are they? Which are good and which not so good, which deliver and which don't? If NGO's were assessed and rated in terms of their delivery and effectiveness, the best would get more support and the others would have to up their game.

What's special about humans? Why should human life be sacrosanct while elephants, rhinos, sharks and the rest of the animal kingdom are considered there to be exploited? Crimes against humanity can be tried in international courts. Crimes against wildlife, are crimes against planet earth, and should come into the same category as crimes against humanity.

The Poacher's Moon

CHAPTER 4 – FIGHT FOR SURVIVAL

In the middle of the morning Lady struggled to her feet. As she rose Pieter and Riaan, a game ranger, noticed the darts hanging from her left side. Riaan put on gloves, removed the darts and handed them to the captain of the investigating Hawks team. The whole area had been cordoned off and as the day wore on Pieter became more and more disappointed with the actions and attitudes of the investigating officials. A constable had been appointed as the lead investigator and she was totally ignorant of this type of crime. Pieter questioned the appointment and let it be known that he didn't think the Hawks were treating the case very seriously or giving it the right level of priority. However, by evening he decided to put aside his concern over police disinterest and concentrate solely on Higgins and Lady.

Higgins was a pitiful sight, and as Pieter sat by the ditch talking to him he fought back tears. He didn't know if Higgins could hear him properly or would be comforted by his voice but he needed to feel he was doing something.

"You haven't eaten anything all day". Bottie sank to his haunches beside his friend and handed him a flask of coffee and sandwiches. "You know Pieter it was a full moon last night". "I know" Pieter replied. "They call it the poacher's moon". They sat till late talking to Higgins and trying to put together the pieces of the puzzle that would help them understand how the attack had been carried out. Bottie was exhausted and just after midnight gave up trying to stay awake and went home to sleep. He would be needed just as much tomorrow and would be useless if he didn't get some rest. Pieter spent the night with his back against a Black Wattle tree whispering to Higgins. From time to time the rhino's ears moved as if in acknowledgement. Pieter told him he had to fight, he couldn't leave Lady alone, and that he, Bottie, Denis the ranger, and everyone at Fairy Glen would fight with him. Before drifting into an uncomfortable sleep Pieter is convinced he heard Higgins cry, it was an almost human noise, and his own cheeks became wet with tears as tiredness overtook him.

———————

The sun rose for the second day after the attack and Pieter woke, swapping his sleeping nightmare for a waking one. Higgins had moved a little during the night which was a good sign and meant he was alive. He looked weird and disfigured. Where only two days ago there had been horns, now there was a flat snout covered in

Stockholm Tar with cotton wool poking out around the edges. Pieter eased his aching joints into action and got up to go and check on Lady. Like Higgins, she was a strange and sad sight. He needed a wash, coffee and something to eat so he trudged wearily up to the lodge.

————————

At the Inverdoorn reserve, Damien Vergnaud hadn't slept all night. In the late morning he got the call he had been dreading. Fairy Glen's rhinos had been attacked by poachers and were fighting for their lives. First Aquila, now Fairy Glen, the curse of rhino poaching was creeping closer and Damien knew he would be next. Inverdoorn is a larger reserve than Fairy Glen and Aquila and its rhinos are free-roaming. Damien knew only too well what dead rhino with their horns removed looked like, and in his mind's eye the vision haunted him. How could he protect his animals? There were various options and he started considering them all.

————————

Bottie and Dennis were with Higgins and Lady by the time Pieter got back from the lodge. Neither rhino had eaten or drunk since yesterday's attack and Lady was too weak to stand for long. Bot flies laying their eggs in the wounds were a serious danger, and all day long Bottie and the reserve staff fought to keep the flies off by spraying the wounds with Vendona. The assault on the rhinos had grabbed the attention of the media, and newspapers, television and radio stations from all over the world had picked up the story. Pieter wanted the right message to get out so handled all the media himself. Between calls from journalists and reporters he was contacted by Archbishop Desmond Tutu, by a distressed elderly lady in Worcester, and had many other sympathy calls from people he'd never even met. As well as condemning the criminals Pieter assured the media and well wishers that he would fight all the way to ensure Higgins and Lady survived.

At the end of the second day Pieter decided to sit up for the second night. He'd had so much support from people he didn't know, he now felt as if he were fighting for them as well. Bottie had brought a camp bed, some coffee and a lantern and then headed home.

The day before the attack there had been fires to the north east of the reserve and the helicopter fire fighters had been sure it was arson. Lying on his camp bed above Higgins in the ditch, Pieter stared at the stars and tried to come to terms with events. This was no random amateur attack, it was carefully planned, and carried out by professionals. The fire had been lit to test his defences, show the watchers how many staff he had, and move the animals to the southwest fence where they would be easy to attack.

Rhino horn is big business and poachers aren't concerned whether the animals live or die. Higgins and Lady were both still alive so they had a chance, and this is what Pieter clung to during his second night of troubled sleep.

In winter the mountain slopes behind Fairy Glen had once been used by snow skiers. Mid-December is high summer and daytime temperatures were getting close to 40 degrees. Lady and Higgins still hadn't eaten or drunk. Regular attempts with water buckets met with no success. They were dehydrating fast and getting weaker by the hour. Bottie built little pools by their heads and wondered whether despite his determination he might lose one or both of the animals.

Most humans don't believe in miracles, but Pieter does. A shadow was creeping over the ground towards him, he looked around and the reserve behind him was no longer covered in sunlight. Clouds were taking over the sky and the air cooled noticeably. Cool went to cold, almost to winter temperatures and the first raindrops fell. This weather was unheard of in summer and Pieter raised his eyes to the heavens and said 'thank you'. Somehow Higgins and Lady had picked up the signal - it wasn't their day to die - and Higgins stretched painfully forward and drank from a little puddle that had formed by his head. While it rained lower down it snowed in the mountains behind. Pieter believes God sent him a miracle. Within an hour both rhinos were on their feet and drinking from puddles. Pieter, Bottie and Denis exchanged grins that split their faces. Before there had been hope and determination, now they were sure that Higgins and Lady would survive!

Apart from brief visits to the lodge Pieter hadn't left his animals for nearly three days. After sleep, food, a shower and a shave it was a new Pieter who arrived back at the reserve just after dawn on the fourth morning. Higgins was standing in the ditch and making noises as if he were calling to Lady. So far each rhino had fought for life without the other. Rhino eyesight is not good, but Higgins' ditch was deep enough to hide him from Lady anyway. Pieter got up and walked towards Higgins who looked as if he was going to try and climb out of the ditch by himself. Pieter, Bottie and Denis had been discussing ways to help him get out of the ditch. Slings, ropes, a heavy lifting vehicle and other equipment were being assembled to help him. It wasn't necessary because, as Pieter watched, Higgins struggled out and stood above the ditch looking confused, as if he didn't know which way to go.

Continued page 49

Lady leans on a tree to help her stay on her feet
copyright Fairy Glen

She collapses back onto the ground with the effort
copyright Fairy Glen

Top and above – Higgins in the dam trying to cool off and cover himself with mud

Continued from page 46

Lady was only a hundred metres away but Higgins went in the opposite direction unaware how close he was to his mate. The distressed animal crashed through bushes and tripped over his own feet as he unknowingly distanced himself from Lady. Pieter wondered whether the trauma had left him totally confused, or whether he was disorientated without his horns, or whether the sun's ultraviolet rays had left him blind. The questions flew through his mind as he watched his friend stumble away and he had no answers.

Lady moved as well and by Thursday morning, four days after the attack, the previously inseparable pair were two kilometres apart at either end of the reserve. The most important thing now was to get them eating again. Bottie had brought bales of hay and they tried with Higgins first. He sniffed it, then tasted it and gently, probably painfully, ate half the bail. Having succeeded with Higgins Pieter and Bottie had high hopes they would also get Lady eating, but she sniffed the hay and walked away. Success came the next day when they resorted to bribery and poured molasses over the top of the bale. She couldn't resist the sweet sugary smell and started eating slowly and with difficulty. Pieter was close enough to be able to see a long deep gash in her upper lip. One of the panga cuts had missed, which was making eating painful.

After six days of struggle Pieter hoped his problems were coming to an end.

For Damien at Inverdoorn the problems were just beginning. The police had now told him they had intelligence that his rhinos would be attacked next. He knew he was in a race against time to take measures to protect his animals. De-horning was a measure used by many but he did not want to disfigure his rhinos. Large scale armed security patrols would work, but would be very expensive and he wouldn't be able to keep it up for long. Penning the rhinos so they could be watched constantly was instantly discounted as these are wild animals and Damien wanted them to be free. He spent long hours on the phone with Alex Lewis, his vet, and slowly another strategy developed. If they could inject the horns with a substance that would remain permanently, and make them impossible to sell, then the poachers would have nothing of value to come and steal.

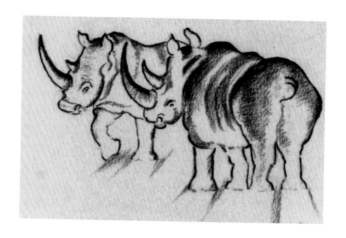

The Poacher's Moon

CHAPTER 5 – THE FAIRY GLEN INVESTIGATION

Higgins and Lady were winning their fight for life and the media storm had passed.

Pieter became obsessed with the question of who had done this and why, where the horns were now, and whether the police would catch the poachers? He wanted answers and he wanted to know what action was being taken.

The initial police presence had looked impressive. A police general, officers of the Hawks specialist crime unit, investigators from Cape Nature and a forensic team had all arrived fast, cordoned off the area and gone about their business. Pieter had given his affidavit to the Hawks captain, and had queried why the investigation was being handled by an inexperienced low-ranking officer. He had been assured the constable would receive help and supervision from experienced senior officers.

Police trackers had worked the ground and discovered the tracks of three men and the place at which they had cut the fence and left the reserve. There was no sign as to where the poachers had entered Fairly Glen. The reserve isn't difficult to access and one suspicion was that one or all three of the poachers might have masqueraded as clients and gone on a game drive, or even stayed at the lodge.

On Wednesday, four days after the attack, Pieter got a call from a friend who is a vet. This contact, who acted in confidence and on the basis his identity would not be disclosed, gave Pieter names of suspects, a description of the vehicle they used, and the location of where the horns might be.

Pieter called the police colonel in Cape Town and was told he was busy with an investigation, but would pass the information to the investigating officer (the constable) who would report progress to Pieter by 0730 hours the next morning. He went to bed hoping the police were acting on the information and he would get news soon.

The next day was taken up with getting Higgins eating again and by evening they remembered they had heard nothing from the police. Suspects names, the description of a vehicle, and even an address, what more did the police need? Pieter began to wish he could take matters into his own hands and do the police job for them. He went home and once again got on the phone. In no uncertain terms he expressed his frustration and disappointment, and demanded to know what use had been made of the information he had passed the police thirty six hours ago. Trails go cold and Pieter knew that it wouldn't be long before this trail was too cold to follow.

His irate phone call produced a reaction and fifteen minutes later Officer Fritz from the Hawks rang him. Fritz had an air of efficiency and competence about him and Pieter felt that at last he had an investigating officer who would make progress. An appointment was made for 0900 hours the next morning.

The new investigating officer was thirty minutes early for the meeting, which started with Pieter quizzing him closely about his experience and background. Pieter himself is an ex-police officer, so when Fritz explained his background in the Murder and Robbery unit in Brixton, Pieter was able to evaluate the calibre of the new man.

Now in possession of all of Pieter's information, Fritz left to follow up the potential leads. The address Pieter had been given for the suspects was in Elands Bay on the West Coast. The police went there and the vehicle was discovered in the garage, but the suspects were not there and there was no evidence to link those who had lived in the house to the poaching of Higgins and Lady. Nearly a week after Pieter had given the information, and a week and a half since the attack, and the trail had gone cold.

Next came a bizarre twist when a relative of one of the suspects – a man known to Pieter – turned up at Pieter's office asking to borrow a small sum of money for petrol. The suspects were small time game dealers working on the fringes of legality. What was one of them doing coming to ask Pieter to borrow a small sum of money? Pieter's suspicion is that the man was trying to show him that he had no money and therefore wasn't part of the gang. Pieter called the police and the man was arrested at the gates of the lodge. Police enquiries revealed that he was wanted for game dealing irregularities in Limpopo province and he was transferred there. Pieter is convinced that had the police investigation moved faster and been more competent the poachers would have been caught. He had given the police hot information from a reliable source and days had been wasted. Ten days after the poaching incident Higgins and Lady were slowly recovering, and Bottie and Pieter's family persuaded him to go on a planned Christmas break.

Pieter had thought the man turning up to borrow money was weird but things got even more strange when, on Christmas Day, he got a call from a man named Mike who said he worked in exports and wanted to talk about the poaching incident. Mike sounded very credible and when he called Pieter for a second time asking him to take a parcel back with him to Worcester (near Fairy Glen) Pieter agreed. The parcel was to be delivered to where the family were staying at seven the next morning. Mike had not made clear whether there was any connection between the parcel and the poaching, and Pieter spent an anxious ten minutes waiting at the gate for it to arrive.

The parcel carrier turned out to be an elderly woman called Suzy and the parcel was a parrot! It appeared that Pieter was merely being asked to do an innocent favour for his potential informant. As he drove back up from the gates with the parrot in its cage on the seat beside him, he found himself trying to talk to it and wondered whether he was going mad. He discussed the police investigation with the parrot, and asked the bird who Mike was but made no more progress with the parrot than he had with the police!

On the drive back to Fairy Glen surrounded by his family he got a 'number withheld' call: "Careful, you're playing with fire and you'll get burnt". The threat was clear but was it in relation to anything specific? Was he being warned off following up with Mike? When they got back to Worcester the parrot was collected by a woman who confirmed a meeting with Mike the next morning at eleven o'clock and gave Pieter the address.

With officer Fritz next to him Pieter was knocking on Mike's door at the appointed time. Mike is blind and he has two false eyes which he took out at the beginning of the meeting saying "My eyes have already been removed because I saw too much". Pieter and Fritz exchanged glances, and Pieter wondered if he had perhaps strayed into a lunatic asylum. However, the fear and the tension that Mike transmitted were real and both men felt it. His eyes were not his only injuries, his arms had light scars and at some time his wrists had been slashed. Mike's troubles had started when he took a new partner into his import/export business in Cape Town. His new partner was Chinese, and Mike had begun to give information to the police about new activities which had started and which worried him. He spoke of not fully trusting the police anymore, and of having handled a rhino horn that was being exported only a week before.

The meeting was tense and disjointed, and Mike said he wouldn't talk unless he was guaranteed immunity from prosecution and given police protection. Officer Fritz pointed out that such guarantees were not easy to get and he needed a lot more hard facts. Mike refused to cooperate further without the protections he had asked for and another trail hit a dead end.

Pieter believes Mike was genuine and had real information of value, but equally he was a muddled and badly frightened man who wouldn't give the police enough to convince them.

Was the blind man aware of the suspects based on the West Coast? Had they poached the horns to order for his Chinese colleagues? The horns weighted approximately eleven kilograms, and at that time rhino horn was ultimately worth around 495,000 rand per kilo. Maybe the poachers had been partners in the venture, or possibly just hired hands. Their night's work could have earned them 5,000 rand each, 50,000, or much more. Pieter and the police still have the questions, but none of the answers.

Author's note: *(When writing this one year and six months after the attack neither Bottie nor Denis or any other staff at the reserve, have been asked by the police to give a statement, and at the time of going to press the rand was worth 9.80 to the US$ and 14.60 to the £ sterling.*

The Poacher's Moon

CHAPTER 6 – TRIALS AND TRIUMPHS

The attack on the Aquila reserve on 20th August sent warning signals to Fairy Glen and Inverdoorn. Both reserves started all-night patrols; but with limited manpower resources, and rangers doing long days with visitors, intense patrolling can only be kept up for so long. With the help of a deliberate arson ploy the poachers had found a chink in Fairy Glen's armour.

Inverdoorn had been running patrols with two vehicles and four rangers since the August Aquila attack and by December, although still fully committed, the rangers were starting to wonder whether perhaps the scourge had passed.

By mid-morning on Sunday 11th December the news that Fairy Glen's rhinos had been poached had reached Inverdoorn, and everyone was back on high alert. Damien Vergnaud was returning to the reserve from Cape Town with a French documentary film crew when he got the news. He and his vet had already decided on a process that would allow the animals to keep their horns but render them valueless. He would now accelerate putting the idea into action. Whatever the cost he had to keep his rhinos safe.

On Sunday night the patrols were out in the reserve and head ranger Wilna Paxton was enjoying a braai (barbeque) with friends on a rare evening off. Just after ten o'clock she realised the zebra were barking like crazy and she sensed something was wrong. Wilna wasted no time: she grabbed her rifle and was in her vehicle and moving in minutes. She headed for the 'viewing tower' which is the highest point on the reserve. She switched off her lights and made her way up the familiar track to the tower. Much of the reserve was visible and her eyes worked their way slowly round three hundred and sixty degrees. The animals, and particularly the zebra, were still restless but she could neither see nor hear anything wrong.

Wilna radioed her patrols who confirmed everything was OK and that they were close to the three rhinos. She reported to Damien at the lodge, decided to stay on watch for a while, and lit a cigarette.

Her eyes strained into the night and she thought she picked up a faint blue light down on the road along the reserve's boundary. Again she radioed the rangers who said they thought she was seeing a light from a house. Wilna knew there was no house there and her nerves jangled as she realised someone with a light was on the road working along their fence. Procedure was that one of the ranger's vehicles conducted mobile patrols, while the other stayed with the rhinos. The patrol with the rhinos radioed in to say something had spooked them and they had taken off. The rangers couldn't follow so were now no longer in touch with the three animals.

Wilna again called Damien to report, but he had already collected his 9mm H & K automatic pistol and was on his way to join her. She cradled her .22 magnum rifle, and realised she might have to shoot at a human before the night was over. The rifle was fitted with a good light-gathering scope, which she used to look for the rhinos and their possible attackers.

.22 is a high velocity calibre, the military .223 (5.56mm) bullet is only very slightly larger. A .22 magnum bullet with a hollow point will pop a human heart like a balloon, and a shot into the head will almost certainly prove fatal. Shooting an animal to end suffering was something Wilna handled with regrets but no qualms, but what would it be like to have a human in the cross hairs? She would follow the rules and first shout a challenge then fire an overhead warning shot. If the poachers didn't either run or surrender, and she felt her life or that of her rhinos was threatened, then she would have to make her decision.

She lit another cigarette and was pleased to note that her hands were steady and her palms dry. She came to terms with her thoughts and knew that if she had to she would pull the trigger.

Damien arrived and stood next to Wilna. They didn't speak, they didn't have to, each understood what the other was thinking. The radio came to life again as one of the ranger teams reported torchlight inside the reserve. There had been a long flash followed by two shorter ones; clearly the poachers were signalling each other. Wilna mobilised every vehicle she had and ordered them into the reserve. She instructed that everyone turn on their hazard lights as a crude but effective means of location and identification.

Caution and silence were no longer necessary. It would have been good to catch the poachers, but the main objective was to let them know they had been sighted, and hopefully frighten them off and keep the rhinos safe. Headed by Damien and Wilna the whole force of over 10 rangers was now in the reserve and frantically looking for the rhinos and the poachers. Damien fired into the air to show the poachers they faced armed opposition.

If you know what you are doing it doesn't take long to dart a rhino and hack its horns off. Damien and the rangers prayed they wouldn't find their animals dead or dying in pools of blood with their horns removed.

Another three flashes, this time in a different place. Were the poachers trying to confuse the rangers, were they testing them or signalling? Headlights were switched on near where Wilna had first seen the lights and a car roared off at high speed. The sound of the vehicle's departure merely heightened the tension. Until the rhinos were found no one would know whether or not the vehicle had left carrying their horns.

The police had been called, were on their way to the reserve, and were setting up roadblocks to cut off the escape routes the poachers might use. The reserve became quiet, and there were no more torch flashes. As the night hours wore on the tension stayed high as successive radio contacts kept on reporting that the rhinos couldn't be found.

By two in the morning Damien had decided his rhinos were either dead or would not be found alive until the morning. At first light the reserve's guests would be up and expecting to go on game drives, so he had to let some rangers get enough sleep to be able to work properly the next day. Sleep was not an option for Damien and Wilna who, together with a pair of rangers, kept up the search all night.

Dawn is spectacular in the Namqua Karoo as the sun's first rays creep over the mountains. As the light increased both vehicles were heading back to the lodge when Damien saw a rhino. The male was standing up, side on, and both its horns were clearly visible. Thirty metres away the female and her calf slept. All three animals were untouched and the sense of relief was as powerful as anything any of them had ever felt before.

The strong suspicion has to be that the same gang who nearly killed Higgins and Lady tried to repeat their poaching at Inverdoorn the next night. The Fairy Glen attack meant Inverdoorn was on high alert and this, together with the zebras' barking, probably saved their rhinos from sharing Higgins and Lady's fate. Damien knew the poachers would try again, the value of rhino horn made that a certainty. For several days the confrontation continued and the poachers tested the reserve. Damien was under constant pressure to cut off his animals' horns as a way of ending the standoff. Cutting the horns off would mean permanent disfigurement of an African icon so he was determined to find another way. The police told him not to drink anything he had not opened himself and he slept with his weapon.

To keep his rhinos safe Damien had to make their horns worthless. However, this in itself was useless unless he could get the word out so that any potential poachers would know that it was a waste of time attacking his rhinos.

Damien and his vet Alex Lewis had decided to inject their rhinos' horns with a triple-action cocktail. The first ingredient was a powerful permanent red dye, the idea being that the consumer was used to rhino horn ending up as a grey powder. If the powder was bright red it would not look like rhino horn powder, indeed it could be anything, so the dealers wouldn't buy it. The second ingredient was an agent that made the horn or the powdered horn fully detectable by x-ray. Of course many smuggled horns don't go through x-ray machines, but enough do to make this ingredient worth including. The third component of the cocktail was a foul tasting substance that would leave a very nasty taste in the consumer's mouth for a long time.

Damien and Alex were confident that the combined effect of the three ingredients would make the horns worthless. The rhinos would have to be darted and the cocktail injected into the horns under pressure in various places. It was vital that the cocktail spread evenly throughout the whole structure which was the reason for the pressurised injection in various places up and down the horns.

The rhinos wouldn't be safe until the horns had been treated and everyone knew about it, so while Alex prepared the cocktail and worked out how to carry out the treatment, Damien worked overtime contacting radio, TV, and the newspapers to ensure the message would get out to the poachers. While the treatment and media coverage was being arranged, the only way to ensure the animals' safety was physical patrolling, so Wilna and her rangers kept them under observation 24 hours a day.

Throughout this period Inverdoorn was a strange place. The public arrived everyday and were taken on game drives as normal and were completely unaware of the frantic activity going on behind the scenes.

Continued on page 69

The gates to Inverdoorn   *copyright Inverdoorn*

Inverdoorn's owner, Damien Vergnaud   *copyright Inverdoorn*

Head ranger Wilna Paxton

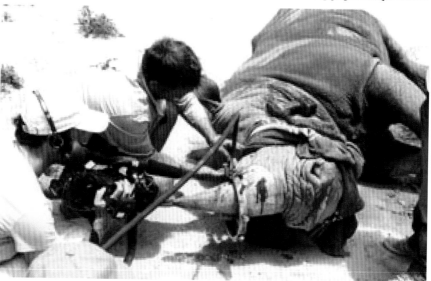

Treating the first rhino

Above and below, infusion treatment in progress   *copyright Inverdoorn*

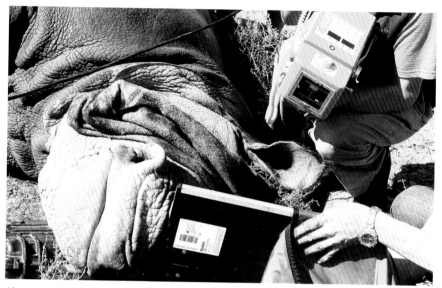

Above and below, the triple ingredient cocktail makes horns x-ray detectable, bright
red in colour and foul tasting *copyright Inverdoorn*

Some weeks after treatment the red dye can still be seen on the surface of the horn

Continued from page 63

There was a palpable air of tension and excitement among the reserve staff and as the days wore on everyone was drawing on adrenalin and determination to keep going. The poachers could return any night and until the rhinos had been treated the team were in a race against time.

While the physical security continued, Damien and Alex Lewis experimented with techniques to find the best way to inject the cocktail under pressure. Alex found some wood with the same density as rhino horn and had several dummy runs to improve the injection technique and ensure effective penetration and diffusion.

By 20th December they were ready and Damien alerted all the media he had been briefing. In addition to the media, officials from Cape Nature and the police were invited to watch the procedure.

The plan was to treat all three rhinos in one day. At 6.00 a.m. on the 23rd Damien, Alex, Wilna and a couple of helpers left the lodge in two vehicles and moved into the reserve. The night patrol had been watching the animals and left as Damien's party arrived. The female and calf would be treated first so that the technique could be practised before the media, police and others turned up to watch. It was soon evident that the days of practising, experimenting and rehearsing had paid off. The animals were darted, went down, and both were successfully treated before being given the antidote. This was a procedure only rarely carried out before, and Damien's team had now perfected and developed it.

By 11.30 the media and others were watching the male rhino being treated and the team were working with confidence and practised efficiency. There was another observer too: Soon after the male had been darted a white helicopter arrived with no identification or registration numbers and blacked out windows. The machine hovered overhead for 2-3 minutes and then left. No markings meant the helicopter was flying illegally and to this day its identity and purpose are mysteries. What only very few people realised was that all along Damien and Alex had a plan B. If for any reason the procedure had not worked on the first two rhinos Alex would have simply cut their horns off before giving them the antidote, and then done the same afterwards with the male.

There were celebrations that night at the lodge, and everyone shared a real hope that perhaps they had developed an effective new weapon in the war against the poachers.

Night falls fast in the Karoo and twilight doesn't last long. The reporters and TV crews had left and were telling the story, and Damien and Alex hoped their actions would prove to be enough to save their rhinos. Only time would tell, and the patrols had to go on until Damien was sure the story was out so that even the dumbest potential poacher knew his rhino horns were valueless. (Note: *The 24 hour surveillance became a permanent part of life on Inverdoorn, which continues to this day.*)

In the immediate aftermath of the rhinos being injected came some bizarre twists. Damien received more than one anonymous death threat. He also received information from the police that he and the rhinos were still a target just to make an example of them, and send a message to other reserve owners that even if they treated their rhinos they would not be safe.

Damien's father is a French explorer and his mother is Spanish. He grew up in the largely unexplored jungles and bush of central east Africa and reacted to the threats to his life and his rhinos with a Gallic shrug and a what will be will be philosophy. He had done all he could and would now call the poachers' bluffs and wait. On police advice he sent his wife and children away from Inverdoorn, but he stayed with his rangers and his rhinos.

The weeks went by and turned into months and there were no attacks and the threats stopped. As the time passed Damien, Wilna and the rangers relaxed the intensity of their security but kept the rhinos under watch every night through the hours of darkness.

The struggle to stop poaching altogether is far from over and is often likened to a war. History may show that Damien and his team not only took part in the war, they may have won a very significant battle by developing their horn treatment cocktail.

Inverdoorn's rhino – safe at the moment   *copyright Jacqui Peirce*

Inverdoorn is also a cheetah rescue centre   *copyright Jacqui Peirce*

The Poacher's Moon

CHAPTER 7 – REUNITED AND RECOVERING

A week after the attack Higgins and Lady were both still in an awful mess. They looked strange without horns and the huge wounds on their faces were a continual reminder to Pieter and the others of the pain they were in. Flies were both a constant irritant and a danger, and one of the main tasks each day was to spray the wounds with Vendona.

Both animals were eating and drinking but this was instinct cutting in to ensure survival, there was no pleasure in their grazing and their eyes spoke of pain, suffering, and confusion. Lady's eyesight didn't seem to have been affected too much by exposure to the sun's rays. This was probably because she had been found first and her vacant, drugged, open eyes were quickly covered with a wet towel. Higgins was found much later and the sun had made him almost blind.

He seemed lost and appeared to have no sense of direction as he plodded wearily round the reserve a long way from Lady. Pieter knew that the rhinos' chances of recovery, and the speed of that recovery, would be greatly helped if he could get them back together. However, they were separated by nearly two kilometres, one animal was blind, the other's sight was OK - but rhino don't have good eyesight anyway, and both were preoccupied with their suffering.

Pieter now developed health problems of his own when he contracted chickenpox. Children often brush this illness off lightly but in adults it can be serious, and Pieter's doctor told him to go to bed for two weeks and avoid exposure to sunlight. Three days later came another emergency call from Fairy Glen – the reserve was on fire! Jan, the reserve manager, told Pieter that helicopters were on the way to help put out the fire and advised Pieter that everything that could be done was being done. Bottie had taken over daily caring for Higgins and Lady so they were in good hands. But as Pieter lay in his darkened room he thought of the near blind Higgins smelling fire and not knowing which way to run. He also thought of the other animals being forced by the fire into the fences. He thought of the panic, the noise, the smoke and his animals, and ten minutes later was dressed and in his vehicle heading for the reserve.

Four helicopters circled the reserve as Pieter hurtled through the gates heading for his second emergency in a month. He saw that the animals were widely scattered but all trying to get away from the flames and the smoke.

Bottie ran up to him as he pulled up at the lodge. "You're crazy Pieter, the doctor told you to stay in bed. There are lots of us here, we can handle this". There is no one in the world that Pieter trusts more but he had to know the answer to his overriding concern: "Where are Higgins and Lady? We must find them".

Bottie knew that would be Pieter's first question. "Lady is safe, and I've got the choppers looking out for Higgins". He had hardly finished speaking when his radio crackled into life and one of the helicopters reported that Higgins was by the dam. It was a relief to know where he was but it wasn't good news. Higgins was virtually blind and would be highly stressed so he could easily run into the water and drown. The whole scene was chaos with vehicles going in all directions, helicopters scooping water from the dam, and all the while the smoke and flames getting nearer. A calm sensible animal with full eyesight would have been at great risk but Higgins was sightless and traumatised.

They drove close to where the rhino stood shaking his head and turning round in confusion. He ran a little way, tripped over his feet and stumbled. Pieter could see his wounds had re-opened and blood was dripping from his face. Then Higgins wasn't alone in his confusion and terror. Pieter hadn't noticed Bottie get out of the vehicle and he was now walking straight up to Higgins talking to him as he approached. As he watched Bottie Pieter thinks he probably stopped breathing – this was very dangerous.

Bottie got to about two metres from the rhino and stood there talking, then he turned his back and, still talking, walked away. Like a tame animal Higgins followed and Bottie led him to safety. The risk had looked insane but as Bottie explained to me later he was fairly confident he could pull it off, and anyway on the spur of the moment couldn't think of anything else to do. "By then Higgins knew me, and I think had started to trust me. I had fed him, watered him, sprayed his wounds, and always talked to him whenever I was close. At that time he couldn't see at all so his sense of hearing and the sounds he heard were his main guide. He knew my voice meant food, water, kindness and treatment. He followed me - I don't think there was anything else he could do." Bottie paused and grinned "Except charge me maybe!"

It was a long hard day but by mid-afternoon the reserve's main buildings were safe as were the animals so Pieter went back to bed.

It was crucial to get Higgins and Lady back together again. They had been a pair before the poaching, and everyone was sure they would aid each other's recovery.

Higgins had followed Bottie so perhaps this tactic could be repeated allowing Bottie to lead Higgins to Lady. The fire and the lack of vision combined to make Higgins recovery much slower than Lady's. He kept walking into trees and bushes which kept opening his wounds. He was a sad and pathetic sight and it wouldn't have surprised anyone if he had decided to simply lie down and die. However as well as the urge to reproduce, the survival instinct is dominant in animals and he wouldn't give up.

Pieter and Bottie sat in the vehicle and watched him for a few minutes then Bottie got out, went to the back of the pick up and took a handful of lucerne. Pieter watched as his friend walked slowly towards Higgins talking as he went. It worked Higgins followed the voice he had come to trust and took occasional mouthfuls of lucerne.

Pieter followed them slowly in the truck as the strange pair made their way across the reserve: a six foot 4 inch human being followed by a hornless rhino acting like a domestic animal. Fairy Glen is small but Higgins and Lady could hardly have been further apart. The distance between them was about two kilometres and it took the odd couple nearly five hours to make their slow way across the reserve. Bottie hadn't been expecting a long trek and was only wearing shorts, sandals, a t-shirt, and no hat. As the hours ticked by the sun took its toll, and by the time Higgins came to an abrupt halt Bottie was badly sunburnt and his feet were painful and blistered.

Higgins had stopped, raised his head, sniffed the air and made snorting and soft mewing sounds. The noises seemed at odds with his bulk, but his whole body language had changed and he seemed charged with life. He carried on making these noises while his head cast about as his nose seemed to be conducting its own search. Bottie backed to the vehicle and he and Pieter watched. Suddenly Lady burst from the bushes and ran towards her mate, their heads met gently and they seemed to kiss while two big men looked on with tears in their eyes.

There is an unavoidable human tendency to interpret animal actions in terms of human behaviour and give animals human emotions and feelings. Perhaps animal emotions are close to ours, certainly in the case of Higgins and Lady their recovery speeded up as soon as they found each other. Lady acted as Higgins eyes, and the once dominant and sometimes aggressive male now meekly followed his partner.

The successful attempt to get the pair together followed many failures, and the reunion came almost a month to the day after the poacher's moon attack. Pieter, Bottie and Denis realised it was vital that Higgins knew Lady was still alive. They collected her dung and took it to him, if she had been lying on lucerne, hay, or anything that might have held her scent they took it to him. Two days before the reunion they had led him to within three hundred metres of Lady. He couldn't see her and she hadn't seen him. He had been led down off the high ground to the road and she was below him by the dam. He wouldn't cross the road and turned back up the hill.

Immediately after the attack the wounds had been sealed with cotton wool and Stockholm Tar. It didn't take the rhinos long to dislodge this and after a couple more applications it was abandoned as a wound-sealing treatment.

Vendona is a spray used to dry out wounds and keep them clean and free of flies. Apart from initially being startled by the hiss of the aerosol, Higgins was very tolerant of his spray treatments - in fact he even seemed to enjoy it. Lady was a different story and to quote Denis "You had to have your running shoes on because she would charge you". They worked out a tactic for spraying Lady which involved enticing her to the front of the truck with the sprayer sitting on the engine. This meant she couldn't easily reach the sprayer and the truck could be rapidly reversed if she charged. As the days went by and became weeks, and then months, both rhinos regained condition and a measure of confidence.

Despite following Lady closely, Higgins blindness meant that he often brushed into trees, bushes and other objects and opened up his wounds. Nevertheless the wounds on both animals were healing. Fourteen months later and the skin had grown back across their faces. The wounds still reopened from time to time and then flies became a danger again. But apart from these accidents the physical healing process had gone better than anyone expected.

Continued on page 83

Fire at the reserve after the attack

Higgins trips over his feet and stumbles as he moves away from the action at the dam

Rhinos hanging on after brutal

Melanie Gosling
Environment Writer

THE two Fairy Glen rhino, whose horns were hacked off by poachers after the animals had been drugged, are still alive after eight days – and game reserve owner Pieter de Jager believes they may pull through.

"The female is looking better. I'm very positive about her. The male is still in danger. He's blind, and I'm hoping it's an infection, but the vet said it would be permanent. He walked alright for two days and then walked in circles.

STRUGGLE: The male rhino from Fairy Glen reserve in Worcester is eating and drinking, but is still in a bad way. A photographer has called for the animal to be put down.

'The female is looking better. I am very positive about her'

stood up and walked straight to the water hole and lay in the water for half the day to cool off.

"Then he stood up and I gave him his lucerne. He ate that and went back to the water," De Jager said.

was the longest rhino have survived after suffering this sort of injury and after being drugged.

"The vets say that others have died after two days.

"I'm in touch with the vet in Thabazimbi who translocated the rhino here, and a local vet."

A local freelance photographer, Cheryl-Samantha Owen, who visited Fairy Glen near Worcester with De Jager on Saturday, believes the animals should be put down.

She described the rhino as "two highly stressed animals and what felt like a circus going on around them".

"We were allowed to go very

right up to the animal which should have been left in peace.

"The rhino was obviously very uncomfortable and attempted to go for him," said Owen, who was photographing the animals for National Geographic.

De Jager then took her and two other photographers to the female rhino where they all followed it into the bush.

Owen said later a vehicle full of tourists had pulled up next to the female rhino.

"The next thing they were all following her into the bush. She got spooked and they turned running full pelt to the

"If he
concerne
taking t
Owen sa:
De Ja
when as
Owen's c
He sa
tioned ar
he had g
assistanc
"That
me speci
her phot
"Whe
she went
rhino th
said.

Hope for cruelly hacked Fairy Glen rhino

Staff Writer

THE critically injured male rhino at Fairy Glen reserve near Worcester, has made it into the new year and took a leisurely mud bath at the game reserve's waterhole on New Year's Day.

The rhino has been on the danger list since poachers drugged the animal in mid-December and hacked both its horns off. Trying to get every bit of horn they could, they hacked so deeply they left two holes in the rhino's head.

The animal became blind after the attack. It is not clear if it will be permanent. Reserve owner Pieter de Jager believes the rhino will regain its sight.

"He's not walking in circles any more or crashing into fences. After the attack his immune system was down, so he will get infections. Also, the small horn normally protects the rhino's eyes from bushes and so on. Now he must get used to walking in the bush with no horn," De Jager said.

painted the wound with a tar mixture to try to prevent it from becoming infected.

"The wound is also dry now. The poachers made two holes in his nose bone, but the skin has grown over one of the holes. They slashed right through the bone into his airway. But he is eating, he is walking around, he sits in the mud, so things are going well with him now."

The female rhino on the reserve was also attacked and dehorned by the poachers, but she recovered more quickly than the male.

At Inverdoorn game reserve near Ceres, the three rhino with "poisoned" horns are behaving quite naturally after the operation to poison their horns 11 days ago.

After the poachers' attack at Fairy Glen, Inverdoorn owner Damian Vergnaud decided to take drastic measures to protect his rhino from attack. He got Hoedspruit wildlife vet Alex Lewis to inject a combination of bright red dye and poison into the horns of the three rhino on his reserve. He hopes this will deter poachers. Most rhino horn is smuggled to Asia, where it is ground up for medicine, although it has no proven medicinal qualities. The poison will not kill, but is designed to make anyone who consumes the ground-up horn feel very sick.

"We got a lot of people phoning about this, and many people believe it is the right solution for small parks," Vergnaud said.

Higgins and Lady found one another at last   *copyright Fairy Glen*

On the road to recovery!   *copyright Jacqui Peirce*

Continued from page 79

The physical wounds will eventually heal completely, but we will never know whether the mental scars will also heal. Higgins and Lady are both disfigured. Without horns they are still rhinos but they look strange. There are elephant and buffalo on the reserve and these animals have had to be placed in bomas to allow the rhinos to wander freely. Rhinos use their horns for defence and to push away potential aggressors. Without their horns Higgins and Lady have no defence against other large animals.

If for millions of years an animal's brain has been wired on the basis of having two horns sticking out there are bound to be effects when they are gone.

Twelve months after the attack Higgins was seen mating with Lady and those at Fairy Glen started hoping this grim story might have a happy ending. The gestation period for rhino is 15/18 months and babies are small so Lady won't show signs of pregnancy until she reaches the late stage of pregnancy.

I visited Fairy Glen several times in February and March 2013 when researching this book. Together with Bottie I got out of the vehicle and was able to get quite close before Higgins started snorting and we backed off. I probably imagined it but it did seem as if the sadness was gone. Higgins seemed to have largely regained his sight, and his old boisterousness and protective behaviour towards

Continued page 85

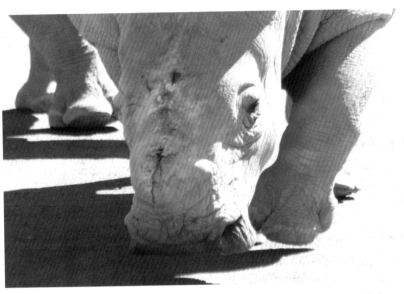

Above and below, they are still rhinos but without their horns they are disfigured

and look strange *copyright Jacqui Peirce*

Continued from page 83

Lady was coming back. Lady seemed more nervous around vehicles and humans so perhaps her mental scars are deeper.

I watched them paddling around in the shallows of the dam and having a glorious mud bath. Human greed has scarred these animals for life, but human love and patience has given them another chance and, though disfigured they look happy once again.

copyright Jacqui Peirce

The Poacher's Moon

CHAPTER 8 – A SPECIES UNDER THREAT – RHINO POACHING

The official figure for the number of rhinos poached in South Africa in 2000, the year Higgins was born, is seven. Thirteen years later as he entered his teenage years that figure had risen to an alarming and staggering 668, and in the first three months of 2013 rhinos were being poached in South Africa at a rate of one every 11½ hours.

Rhinos were hit hard by trophy hunters throughout the last century and by the early 1960's most of the few remaining wild white rhinos lived in what is now South Africa's Kwa Zulu Natal park. The white rhino was largely saved from extinction by South Africans Ian Player, vet Toni Harthoorn and other dedicated conservationists who acted effectively during the 1960's to save the species. By the time Higgins was born the population had recovered to about 20,000 animals, but that was as good as it would get.

The table below gives the poaching figures since 2000. At the time of writing (mid 2013) the annual birth rate still exceeds the numbers being killed by poachers. But if poaching continues at anything like its recent rate of increase the tipping point will soon be reached, and then it's downhill towards extinction again.

POACHING INCIDENTS
(White rhino – South Africa)

2000 - 7
2001 - 6
2002 - 25
2003 - 22
2004 - 10
2005 - 13
2006 - 24
2007 - 13
2008 - 83
2009 - 122
2010 - 333
2011 - 448
2012 - 668
2013 - 446 (up to July 31)

(The above are official figures released by the Department of Environmental Affairs)

In 1993, the People's Republic of China announced a total ban on the sale, purchase, import, export and ownership of rhino horn. Shop owners, dealers, and stockists were given six months to dispose of their stock. Perhaps most importantly rhino horn was removed from the list of state- sanctioned medicines.

The Chinese measures worked and contributed to rhino poaching staying at low levels until 2002 when there was a sudden fourfold increase on the year before, coinciding with Vietnam becoming the main user of rhino horn in the world. By no means all rhino horn that ended up in Vietnam was poached: a significant part was acquired legally. Permits to hunt rhino were issued to trophy hunters who then exported their trophies quite legally, covered by CITES (Convention on International Trade in Endangered Species of wild fauna and flora) permits. By 2010 seventy percent of trophy hunters shooting rhino in South Africa were Vietnamese.

These "legal" hunts enabled unscrupulous operators to run rings around the law and made a mockery of CITES "protection". The transformation of Vietnam's economy since the end of the war with the United States was dramatic. As with the other Asian "tigers", consumer spending power rose and as a result some species of wildlife suffered and came under ever-increasing pressure. One of the worst affected animals was the rhino.

By early 2013 the value of rhino horn was $65,000 a kilo which makes it as valuable as many precious metals and the most expensive narcotics. The higher the value the greater the risks people will take. Poachers know they risk being shot by armed rangers, and thieves are even prepared to poach horns from rhino in zoos and from dead rhino in museums. As Anthony Lawrence puts it in his book "The Last Rhinos" –"If you truly want to grasp the situation faced by conservationists, do what a poacher does and look at a rhino and see a 3ft long horn made of pure gold. Game rangers are in the unenviable and extremely hazardous position of trying to protect solid gold. What should be locked securely in a vault, instead walks around on four legs in the bush".

Rhinos have been walking around in the bush for 50 million years but it's only in the last few years that they've been doing so with a lump of gold stuck on their heads!

There are basically two types of poachers, the simple subsistence level tribesman/hunter who is hunting for the pot or killing for someone else, and the sophisticated highly-resourced criminals using helicopters, dart guns and advanced communications equipment. Very often of course the former works for the latter.

When yesterday's trophy hunters reduced white rhino numbers to less than 500 in the 1960's, the black rhino was healthier at 65,000 – 70,000, but by the end of the 1980's poachers had taken a terrible toll and black rhino numbers were down to around 5,000. Today it is estimated the figure is less than 3,000.

South Africa and Zimbabwe are the main sources of horn, and in recent years poaching in Zimbabwe has returned to levels not seen since the 1980's. At least 123 rhino were poached in 2008, which was the highest number recorded since 1987. The methods used and actions taken by many of the poaching gangs indicated military training, and the AK47 was a favourite weapon for Zimbabwe's poachers.

In researching this book I have read several accounts of rhino poaching and spent hours 'googling'. Among all the books I have read, Julian Rademeyer's *Killing for Profit* stands out as an excellent piece of investigative journalism, which has resulted in more rhino poaching facts and figures in one place than I have found anywhere else. *The Poacher's Moon* in no way sets out to be a definitive work on rhino poaching. My book is essentially the story of the two animals which survived attacks in the Western Cape, and the others which didn't. For the serious student of rhino poaching I unreservedly recommend Rademeyer's book.

I mention this as many of the facts and figures contained in this chapter were sourced from *Killing for Profit*.

In 1977 CITES imposed an international trade ban on rhino horn. In 1978 South Africa reported the export of 149.5 kg of rhino horn to Hong Kong. Further indications of South African government complicity in rhino horn trafficking came in 1982 when Dr. Esmond Bradley Martin published his book *Run Rhino Run*. The 149.5 kg declared in 1978 were shown as having originated from the Natal Parks Board. However records in Hong Kong, Taiwan, and Japan show another 860 kg as having entered these countries from South Africa.

The Natal Parks Board had been a main supplier of rhino horn but stopped selling after 1978 in order to comply with the CITES ban. By the end of 1979 most South African provincial authorities were officially prohibiting the export of rhino horn. However, Japanese records show that in 1980, three years after the CITES ban, 587 kg were imported into Japan from South Africa. The origins of this horn were thought to be Angola, Namibia, Zambia and Tanzania. Whatever the origin, South Africa was part of the routing and these records indicate the regrettable ineffectiveness of international agreements. As with everything throughout the history of both legal and illegal commerce, the reality is "whenever there is a demand there will be a supply".

In *Killing for Profit* Rademeyer shows just what a dirty business rhino horn poaching and trafficking was and still is.

In recent history individuals in African and Asian governments, the governments themselves, game rangers, park wardens, vets and even conservation NGO's looked the other way, or didn't look at all, while animals were slaughtered in increasing numbers.

In the late 1980's Dr. John Hanks was the head of the WWF's Africa programmes. Hanks was an internationally respected biologist and conservationist with a doctorate from Cambridge. In 1981 he was with the WWF's president, Prince Bernhard, in Nigeria. The Prince was dismayed to learn of the extent of rhino poaching at the time and its catastrophic effect on populations. While millions of dollars were being spent on security, very little was being spent on investigating those involved in the actual trade. Prince Bernhard indicated to Hanks that he would like to finance an exercise to track down and expose the smugglers. The Prince stressed that he would fund this himself as he believed it was not appropriate that it be seen as a WWF project, or that the money go through WWF accounts. A noble and sensible approach but possibly also a naive one. The idea came from the WWF President, and was progressed by its head of Africa programmes, so there was no way this exercise would ever be seen as anything other than something the WWF had a hand in.

At the end of 1987 Hanks flew to London to meet the former *SAS founder Sir David Stirling. Sir David was running a private security and intelligence company called KAS Enterprises, whose employees were almost exclusively ex members of the SAS. KAS were eventually contracted to set up operations in Southern Africa to investigate and expose the illegal trade in rhino poaching. The exercise became known as 'Operation Lock' and ran for a few years under the control of the KAS managing director, Colonel Ian Crooke.

*(*SAS. The UK's elite force, the Special Air Service)*

According to ex South African security branch policeman Mike Richards, between February and July 1990 Lock's team sold 98 rhino horns to smugglers. Throughout its time in operation there were claims that 'Operation Lock' was dealing in ivory and rhino horn. If these claims are true it is likely the explanation would be that it was a necessary part of their intelligence gathering and infiltration operations. Whatever the excuse or explanation, it is astonishing that an outfit which had been instigated by senior figures in the WWF should be dealing in animal products.

It was a shadowy world, inhabited by shadowy people who were comfortable living in the shadows. It is unlikely that full details of KAS operations and all those involved in them will ever come out. What we can be sure of however is that the WWF, and agencies in both the British and South African governments, must have had a good idea of what was going on.

There are those who believe that the end justifies the means and that 'Operation Lock' had some success. I have even heard it claimed that Lock was partly responsible for the reduction in poaching during the 1990's, but I suspect the Chinese ban in 1993 had more to do with it.

————

As the number of rhinos being poached grew since 2003, so did the number of Vietnamese 'hunters' coming to South Africa to hunt them in order to procure their horns as trophies. South African government records show that in 2003 at least 20 rhino horns were exported to Vietnam, (there were nine trophies - both horns - and two single horns). In 2005 the figure was 12 trophies (24 horns), in 2006 the number had increased to 146 horns, in 2008 it went down again to 98, then 136 in 2009, and 131 in 2010.

This hunting done on permit allows horns to be kept as trophies and exported by the hunter under the cover of a CITES trophy certificate. In the seven years between 2005 and 2010 at least 659 horns were taken in this way. Using average horn weights this means that a staggering 2 to 3 tonnes of rhino horn was legally exported to Vietnam. This produces a black market value of between $200 and $300 million, while the trophy fees would only have come to $20 million. This wasn't just a legal anomaly, it was a loophole you could fly a jumbo jet through and the profits were huge.

The CITES treaty is often hailed as being the only effective barrier between many species and their extinction. CITES Appendix 1 and II listings have had their successes, but as we have seen with rhino the system is open to abuse, and without the conscientious compliance of member states its effectiveness will remain limited. Controlling, limiting, and banning trade in endangered species is supposed to promote sustainability; it would do if it worked, but while the abusers (individuals, organisations, and governments) can operate largely unchecked, CITES will remain an expensive good idea.

The CITES treaty came into effect in July 1975 and South Africa was a founding member, China ratified it in 1981, Thailand in 1983, Vietnam in 1994 and Laos in 2004. All the main nations involved in the rhino horn trade are CITES members. The green movement often calls CITES "the animal dealers' charter", and many animal rights activists claim it promotes trade rather than stops it!

In 1994 South Africa proposed changing the white rhino CITES listing from Appendix I (threatened with extinction) to Appendix II (trade to be strictly regulated). The conference members allowed this and, as we have seen, 'hunting' operations eventually played a major part in supplying Vietnam's horn market after 2003.

By 2012 the Vietnamese hunters had all but disappeared, but had started to be replaced by hunters from Eastern Europe, notably Poland and the Czech Republic. These new "sportsmen" and women were being recruited by the Vietnamese horn dealers, who were offering paid for holidays in South Africa in return for names on licence applications and the presence of the licence holders when the animals were shot.

The Boere Mafia was the name for an Afrikaans-speaking organisation which was involved in hunting safaris, and allegedly in canned hunting, and poaching. Members of the organisation were accused of various offences including rhino horn poaching.

However, in October 2010 the case against them was thrown out of court on the grounds that the charges stemmed from arrests made four years earlier, and the prosecution case was largely based on the questionable testimony of a convicted felon. (It is suspected that this witness was a member of the gang and was frightened into not testifying).

Following a fifteen month investigation called 'Project Cruiser', Dawie Groenewald and accomplices found themselves, in late 2011, facing 1,872 counts of racketeering, money laundering, fraud, intimidation, illegal hunting and dealing in rhino horns. Dubbed the Groenewald Gang, Dawie and his ten co-accused, which included his wife, other professional hunters, veterinarians, safari operators, and a helicopter pilot have so far managed to delay their case being heard.

The gang first appeared in court in September 2011 and there have subsequently been a number of postponements. They appeared in court in October 2012 and the case was adjourned until May 2013. In May it was decided that the case would be heard in the High Court in Pretoria in July 2014. Some conservationists fear that the Groenewald Gang prosecution may end up going the same way as the Boere Mafia case, with charges either being dropped or greatly watered down.

The diplomatic bag has long been used by embassies to move things in and out of host countries which would often be illegal. In strict Moslem states where alcohol is prohibited, the 'dip bag' often enables diplomats to enjoy a glass of wine with dinner. So it is with rhino horn: the bag provides smuggling with impunity.

In mid-2008 Tommy Tuan was arrested by the police at a hotel in Kimberley. He had just taken delivery of rhino horn and in his room was over 20 kg of horn, a handgun, ammunition and a large amount of cash.

Tommy was using a Honda car which was parked in the hotel car park. The vehicle had a diplomatic number plate and its registered owner was Pham Cong Dung, the political counsellor at the Vietnamese Embassy. Two years prior to this incident the police had obtained evidence that the embassy's economic attaché, Nguyen Khanh Toan, was using the diplomatic bag to smuggle horns out of South Africa to Vietnam. Dung's Honda was impounded by the police but later returned after Dung had given the explanation that his car had been borrowed by Nguyen Khanh Toan.

Later in November 2008 TV footage showed an embassy official receiving a number of horns from a known trafficker. The footage was shot outside the embassy and Dung's Honda was parked close by. The person who received the horns was Ms Vu Moc Anh, who was the Embassy's first secretary. The Ambassador told a newspaper that Ms Vu Moc Anh was helping friends and wasn't involved in horn smuggling. Normally Dung's Honda would have been parked inside the Embassy, and his explanation for it being parked outside was that he wasn't using it that day. Vu Moc Anh was recalled to Hanoi to explain her part in the incident, and Dung left South Africa some while later. Despite the evidence that Embassy staff were involved in handling rhino horn, no action was taken by the South African government, seemingly because it wanted to avoid damaging diplomatic relations.

The record of the South Africa authorities bringing successful poaching convictions is poor, and when convictions are obtained the punishment is often hardly a deterrent. However when poachers appeared before presiding magistrate Prince Manyathi in 2010 and 2011 leniency was not on display for Xuan Hoang who was a Vietnamese courier caught at O.R Tambo airport (Johannesburg) in March 2010. Manyatti gave him ten years without the alternative option of a fine. Then in 2011 Doc Manh Chu and Nguyen Phi Hung, who had been arrested at the time of the World Cup, also came before Manyathi. He handed down sentences of twelve and eight years, once again with no option of fines. Conservationists and pro-wildlife activists and campaigners applauded the sentences.

Bilateral talks between South Africa and Vietnam took place in September 2011. It was announced that the parties had agreed to work towards an MOU (Memorandum of Understanding) which would include collaboration on wildlife protection, law enforcement and the management of natural resources. The MOU was eventually signed fifteen months later on December 10th 2012. According to official figures, in the first seven months of 2013 446 rhinos had been poached, which works out to one rhino every 11½ hours. If this rate continues throughout 2013, by the end of the year 766 rhinos will have been poached in the twelve months following the signing of the MOU.

———————

Vietnam may have taken over from China as the world's leading consumer of rhino horn, but Vietnam is by no means the only country involved in this trade. In the 60's and early 70's Hong Kong was a leading player, then between 1970 and 1977 Yemen recorded receiving 22.5 tons of horn which represented 7800 dead rhino. Taiwan was a significant consumer but China with her huge population was at the centre of the trade until their ban came into force.

Today the Lao People's Republic, Thailand, Cambodia, Hong Kong and Taiwan may not account for as much rhino horn as Vietnam, but all these countries are traders and/or consumers.

The Poacher's Moon

CHAPTER 9 – MEDICINE AND MYTH, DELICACY AND DEATH

What is it that makes rhino horn so valuable, worth killing for, and worth taking the risk of dying for? At the heart of the issue is 2000 years of culture and belief. Today we have rapidly dwindling wildlife resources and ever increasing demand from Southeast Asian markets for animal products used in traditional medicine. The rapid recent emergence of Asian economies is producing a consumer market that could prove the death knell for many species.

Sharks are being harvested at a rate of up to 70 million a year which for many species is proving unsustainable. Ivory, lion bones, tiger body parts, rhino horns, and many other animal products are being gobbled up by countries who use them in medicine and as ornaments.

In Arabia and particularly in Yemen and Oman rhino horn was prized as a material for making jambiya and khanjar dagger handles. In Vietnam 9000 health centres practice traditional medicine and most state hospitals have departments which specialise in it. For medicinal use the horn is ground down in special dishes, has water added, and is drunk by the consumer. 0.5 to 1 gram daily is recommended to assist with healing and reducing pain. A Vietnamese pharmacopeia lists rhino horn for treating headaches, fever, delirium and convulsions.

Various rhino products are supposed to act as aphrodisiacs, male performance enhancers, temperature reduction and hangover treatments, and cures for arthritis, back pain and many other ailments. For many reasons cancer is a huge killer in Vietnam, and when a senior government official claimed that rhino horn had cured his cancer the demand for horn rocketed.

According to the World Health Organisation (WHO) up to 200,000 people in Vietnam are diagnosed with cancer each year, and there are 75,000/100,000 cancer deaths annually. The country has a population of about 90 million and the government is simply not capable of treating all of its cancer sufferers. Treatment is expensive, hospitals are overcrowded, and equipment is often antiquated. Little wonder then that when word goes round that rhino horn is a miracle cancer cure desperate patients and their families will obtain it if they can.

Scientists and conservationists make convincing cases showing that rhino horn has little or no medicinal value. But as long as practitioners prescribe it and patients believe in it there will be a demand. Two thousand years of traditional medicine is even more convincing when backed up by today's internet world when a minister claims a cure and the news of it goes viral.

There was a common and mistaken belief that rhino horn was made of hardened hair, but the process is quite different. Actually it is made up of cells that grow out from the surface of the skin of the nose. The cell tubules harden and connect together. The horn is composed largely of the protein keratin which is the same type of protein that makes up human hair and nails, horses hooves and chicken claws.

The ability of rhino horn to help with or cure human ailments may be a myth, but until the myth can be successfully countered it will be responsible for the deaths of increasing numbers of rhinos and their possible slide to extinction.

The Poacher's Moon

CHAPTER 10 – THE WAR AGAINST POACHING

I have many times heard the phrase 'it's a war out there' used to describe the struggle against rhino poaching. It's an accurate description: weapons are being used, armies are involved, and people are being killed.

In Chapter 8 we saw that past members of the British SAS, one of the world's elite military units, were involved in 'Operation Lock' in the late 1980's/early 1990's. This was a covert operation set up to gather intelligence about illegal rhino horn trafficking.

Firearms and military personnel are not the only 'weapons' deployed against the poachers. In the mid 1980's Ed Hearn, the founder of the Krugersdorp Lion and Rhino Nature Reserve, developed a procedure to infuse the horns of rhino with a pink dye and a pesticide. The technique was later further developed and used by Alex Lewis and Damien Vergnaud on the Inverdoorn Game Reserve in 2011. (see chapter 6)

Horns are only worth poaching because of their high value. Making them valueless is an effective way of protecting rhino. Obviously infusing horns only works as a deterrent if it is known that a specific animal or group of animals has been treated. Reserves using this technique must use every possible opportunity to put the word out. Promotional leaflets, advertising, signage at the reserve, merchandise (t-shirts etc.) and advertising must all carry the message "The horns of all our rhino have been poisoned, coloured, and are x-ray detectable". Reserves that follow this procedure could group together in an association and ensure that a list was published and widely distributed identifying those reserves with treated rhino.

The horn infusion procedure is not a foolproof cure for rhino poaching. There are those who claim that the dye and other ingredients disperse within months, but veterinary and scientific experts don't all agree and many think it remains indefinitely in fully mature animals. What is certainly true is that the treatment will need repeating every few years. In places like the Kruger National Park where a large number of animals are dispersed throughout a large area (the Kruger is the size of Israel), there will be issues not only finding the rhino, but then permanently marking them to identify the treated animals. It probably could be done, but it would be a huge and expensive operation which wouldn't negate the need for other measures such as anti-poaching ranger patrols. It is likely therefore that the infusion option recently refined by Vergnaud and Lewis of Inverdoorn will be of most use on relatively small reserves with small numbers of rhino. Vergnaud, Alex Lewis and others have set up 'The Rhino Protect Foundation'. The Foundation is completely independent of the Inverdoorn Reserve, and was created to pass on the expertise the Inverdoorn team has developed.

The Foundation is talking to, working with, and aware of a growing number of reserves including SANParks (Kruger and others) Sabi Sand, Gondwana, Garden Route, Timbauati and others who have already adopted this procedure, or are considering doing so.

Darting rhino and removing their horns has long been considered an effective option but it has several drawbacks. Darting can be a risky business as vet Alex Lewis pointed out to me. In human medicine an anaesthetist carefully assesses patients before they are put to sleep to be operated on. Animals have no such assessments so consequently the risk is higher. When horns are removed the stubs remain and with today's high value even these stubs can be worth the risk of killing a rhino. Finally, horns do grow back so, like infusion, removal is not a permanent measure.

Armed anti-poaching patrols are of limited effectiveness which is proved by the fact that each year armed anti-poaching activities have increased but so has the number of rhinos being killed. In *Killing for Profit* Rademeyer quotes Ken Maggs, the head of SAN Parks ECIS unit: "Last year (2011) we killed twenty one people.

This year, it is about seven so far. Shooting people doesn't solve the problem at all. But you have to be aggressive". Maggs commented further, "All of the guys shot in the park have been in armed conflict. We can't just go and shoot somebody for the sake of shooting somebody. We are bound by laws, whereas the poachers are bound by no rules. A poacher can come in, see one of my guys and kill him. If he gets away with it, he gets away with it. These are armed aggressors coming across our border. Nobody asked a Mozambican to come across. At any one time there are ten to fifteen groups of poachers operating in the park in different areas, all armed with a multitude of weapons. They can come in a group of five, each armed with three weapons, and engage the rangers who – funnily enough – also have families and also live in communities and will be as sorely missed by their families and communities as the poachers are by theirs. We've had hundreds of thousands of people crossing the border from Mozambique into Kruger, and there is certainly no trend of us going out of our way to shoot people. The refugees who come through the park don't come through armed. So if you're coming through with an AK-47, what exactly is it that you're wanting to do?"

Continued page 115

Clear warnings to poachers on the Inverdoorn perimeter fence that the reserve's
rhinos have all been treated and so their horns are valueless

copyright Jacqui Peirce

Treating the horns with the triple ingredient cocktail   *copyright Inverdoorn*

A dart gun, panga, feather darts and anaesthetic similar to those used in attack

copyright Fairy Glen

The AK47 a favourite weapon used by poachers

Perhaps rather a drastic approach but many would agree   *Jacqui Peirce*

Hunting loopholes to be closed

O SAVE RHINO

Illegal wildlife
trade is seen by
criminals as
being low-risk
and high-profit

International crime behind rhino losses

Mari Friday
Tony Weaver

Interpreter in
rhino horn case
'compromised'

WARDA MEYER

Charges
against pair
are likely to
be reinstated

Young rhinos' tiny horn stumps did nothing to
protect them against sophisticated poaching gang

Crime, poaching means fees soar

R1m reward offered for rhino poaching mastermind

Reserve slammed for 'rhino hunt'

Runner bares all to raise rhino awareness

Zara Nicholson
Metro Writer

POISON INJECTED INTO HORNS

Drastic bid to save rhinos

Melanie Gosling
Environment Writer

A WESTERN CAPE game reserve owner has resorted to desperate measure...

NEWS   5

Criminals' new ploy to obtain rhino horn

Tony Carnie

CRIMINAL syndicates have been coping in huge numbers from the Czech Republic, Poland and Slovakia to stop smuggling South Africa's rhino...

CLOSURES: Wildlife vet Alex Lewis injects a mixture of dye and poison into the horn of this drugged rhino on Inverdoorn Game Reserve near Ceres. The operation... Picture: MATTHEW

SA to propose legalising trade in rhino horn at Cites

Sipokazi Fokazi
Political Bureau

SOUTH AFRICA may legalise the trade in rhino horn if it convinces the international community to lift a ban on it...

WWF has said legalising the trade would increase poaching

...

Runner bares all to raise rhino awareness

Zara Nicholson
Metro Writer

STARK naked except for a red rhino horn covering his proboscis, a Cape Town anti-poaching activist has streaked the speeding Kloof Nek...

CHEEKY CAMPAIGN: A screen grab of Steve Newman's YouTube video of him running naked down Kloof Nek Road as part of his campaign to raise awareness about rhino poaching.

2 rhinos killed in sad start to 2013

Angelique Serrao

JOHANNESBURG: Two rhinos have been killed in the first week of the new year...

114

Continued from page 109

As Maggs pointed out, soldiers, rangers and other government employees are bound by rules of engagement – whereas the poachers can do what they like. This means the criminals will always have the advantage as they can be proactive, while anti-poaching forces have to be reactive.

On reserves where the horns have been infused physical security has, in some cases, been reduced but nowhere has it been abandoned altogether. This indicates that for anti-poaching efforts to be effective private rhino owners and SANParks will have to combine a variety of strategies.

I have met many rangers employed by the government (SANParks) and by private reserve owners, and have nothing but respect for these men and women who are on the front line of a real shooting war. They are heroes who are largely unsung so I would like to salute them here. The high value of rhino horn has inevitably led to corruption and rangers have not been exempt, but I do believe the majority of rangers and guides are dedicated to the welfare of the wildlife they work with.

There are many who think the best way to protect rhino is to stop or limit the illegal trade (poaching) by replacing it with a legal trade. Rhino can be farmed by removing horn from live captive animals as the horns re-grow. It can also be removed from dead animals from both wild and captive stocks, and this could produce legal stockpiles of horns. Detractors believe that while increased supply from legal sources might depress values, it would only increase demand; while those in favour argue that a carefully controlled legal supply of horn would undermine the illegal one.

South Africa will host the next CITES meeting in 2016 and according to Edna Molewa, the Water and Environmental Affairs Minister, may present a case for being allowed to sell horn in a legal trade: "Depending on the amount of thinking we will have done by 2016, we could put trade back on the agenda, or we could do it at the one thereafter in 2019. We can't take short cuts!"

The debate on how best to save the rhino is complex and the issues are many. Whilst there are no simple, one-size-fits-all answers and no quick fixes, there are some certainties.

- If the present rate of increase in poaching continues rhinos will once again be threatened with extinction.

- For CITES to be effective it needs to be given some teeth to punish member nations which transgress. The future of, and guardianship of, the world's wild fauna and flora really should be in the hands of the UN or an international body set up by the UN, and given effective policing and sanction capabilities.

- To save the remaining rhinos we must utilise a combination of all the weapons in the armoury – armed anti-poaching patrols, horn infusion, increased public awareness in consumer markets, a controlled legal supply, and strict enforcement of internationally agreed measures. We must also work to curb and stop demand. If there is no demand there will be no supply and rhinos will be safe.

I have no doubt we could save the rhino if we wanted to. The question is, will we?

The Poacher's Moon

EPILOGUE

In writing The Poacher's Moon I have tried to give readers a brief insight into the brutal world of rhino poaching in South Africa, a world driven by avarice and mistaken human belief. But it is really the story of two rhinos, Higgins and Lady. Theirs should normally be a parallel world of grazing, reproducing, sunshine and seasons, and the natural cycles of life and death.

In 2011 Higgins and Lady's natural world collided with man's destructive greed-fuelled way of life. For the rhinos the result of this clash was a new world of pain, blood, blindness, suffering and a mighty struggle to survive. In the end they prevailed. I believe there is a lesson here for mankind, which is that ultimately Mother Nature will always win. Like humans the world has to breathe. If we continue to rip out the world's lungs which are the African and South American rain forests, we are moving down the path of disaster. While scientists debate whether climate change is manmade or a natural cycle, we continue on our largely unchecked rush to deplete the planet's natural resources past the tipping point. In their little world of Fairy Glen, Higgins and Lady are unaware of what humans are doing to the planet. Rhinos have lived on earth for more than fifty million years compared to mans' span of less than half a million. If rhinos can survive the current poaching onslaught and hang on until Mother Nature strikes back, they may well still be around in another fifty million years, long after man has caused his own destruction.

If, when you are born, your brain is wired to the development of two large horns which will grow out of the front of your head, then your brain will have to adjust to their removal. Higgins and Lady's scars have healed now but they will be disfigured for life. I am scribbling this watching them at Fairy Glen where they have just had a paddle in the dam before going to lie down in the shade.

They look happy again now and I hope they are. Locked in their brains are the secrets as to whether they are really happy, whether they still harbour mistrust towards humans, and whether they still miss their horns. There may be another secret locked in Lady's brain. She has been seen mating with Higgins, and she knows whether she is pregnant and may soon be able to raise a finger to the poachers and say, "You did your worst, one day you'll be punished, and I look forward to it, in the meantime ....we won."

———

GLOSSARY, ABBREVIATIONS AND ACRONYMS

CANNED HUNTING - Animals bred or supplied for controlled hunting in small areas

CRASH - A group/herd of rhino

BAKKIE - Pickup truck

BRAAI - B.B.Q

ANC - African National Congress

CITES - Convention of International Trade in Endangered Species of Wild Fauna & Flora

DA - Democratic Alliance

SANParks - South African National Parks

DEA - Department of Environmental Affairs

ECIS - Environmental Crime Investigation Services

FYNBOS - Natural heath/shrubland

JAMBIYA - Yemeni dagger

PANGA - Long broad bladed African knife

MOU - Memorandum of Understanding

SAS - Special Air Service

WHO - World Health Organisation

THANKS AND ACKNOWLEDGEMENTS

Anne Albert

Lawrence Anthony – author – 'The Last Rhinos'

Aquila Game Reserve

Johan Botma

Trevor Carnaby – author – 'Beat About The Bush'

Wilfred Chivell

Tim Davison - editor

Searl Derman

Fairy Glen Game Reserve

Denise Headon – secretary – worn out typing fingers

Inverdoorn Game Reserve

Pieter de Jager

Mandi Jarman

Stanley Kerr

Madelein Marais

Esmond Bradley Martin

Wilna Paxton

Denis Pothas

Julian Rademeyer – author – 'Killing For Profit'

Damien Vergnaud

Clive & Anton Walker – authors – 'The Rhino Keepers'

Brenda Walters

Proof Readers – Jane, Karen, Ken and Glenys